THE DEAD
IN DAYLIGHT

The Dead In Daylight

Melody S. Gee

Cooper Dillon

Acknowledgments

Thanks to the editors of the following journals, where these poems first appeared, sometimes in different forms:

Boxcar Poetry Review: "Why We Are This Way"; *The Collagist:* "The Sea Wall"; *Connotation Press;* "Overwintering," "Swallows in Harbin"; *Construction:* "Or Am I," "Yolk"; *failbetter:* "Los Angeles Pastoral," "A Phrase by Rote," "Sparrow"; *Fox Chase Review:* "The Dead in Daylight"; *Los Angeles Review:* "Bat Exclusion"; *Meridian:* "On The Vine"; *Pilgrimage:* "As If," "A House of Paper and Gut"; *Spillway:* "Hear Her Say Everything"; *Stone's Throw Magazine:* "In Us the Unused"; *Town Creek Poetry:* "I Cannot Make a Torch of Green Branches," "A Womb Sound," "Infertility." Thanks to Jehanne Dubrow and Lindsay Lusby, editors of *The Book of Scented Things Anthology,* where "Gravid" first appeared.

Thank you to Juan J. Morales for your careful, generous readings, and for your constant friendship. Thank you to my fellows at Kundiman, who continue to give me inspiration, support, and community many years after my first poetry retreat. Thank you to my parents and to my Lynch family. Thank you to Bea and Josie for everything good. Thank you to Paul for holding us all in the unbroken orbit of your love, and thank you for every word, especially *yes.*

The Dead In Daylight
Copyright © 2016 by Melody S. Gee
All rights reserved
First edition
Cooper Dillon Books
San Diego, California
CooperDillon.com

Cover Art & Design:
ISBN-13: 978-1-943899-01-2
Shapiro, Harvey. "The Heart" from *National Cold Storage Company* © 1988 by Harvey Shapiro
    Reprinted with permission of Wesleyan University Press
Shaunessy, Brenda. Excerpt from "Hearth" from *Our Andromeda.* © 2012 by Brenda Shaunessy
    Reprinted with permission of The Permissions Company, Inc. on behalf of Copper
    Canyon Press, www.coppercanyonpress.org

Printed in the United States

Table of Contents

I

I Cannot Make A Torch Of Green Branches   3
A Womb Sound   4
A House Of Paper And Gut   5
Los Angeles Pastoral   6
The Sea Wall   8
In Us The Unused   9
Subject To Wind   11
Infertility   13
Sparrow   14
On The Vine   15
Of What Next   16
Yolk   17
Swallows In Harbin   18
Why We Are This Way   19
A Phrase By Rote   21
An Eye To See   24
Gravid   25

II

Go Back, Make Ready   31
The Dead In Daylight   35
Trails   37
Overwintering   39
Rhythms   40
A Sea Beneath Skimming Birds   41
All The Letters   42
Open Field And Mirror   43
The Chain Follows The Light   44
As If   46
Or Am I   47
The Father Collapes   48
Bat Exclusion   49
Hear Her Say Everything   51
A Story Of Bone   54

for Beatrice and Josephine

In the midst of your words your wordless image
Marches through the precincts of my night
And all the structures of my language lie undone:
The bright cathedrals clatter, and the moon-
Topped spires break their stalk.
Sprawled before that raid, I watch the towns
Go under. And in the waiting dark, I loose
Like marbles spinning from a child
The crazed and hooded creatures of the heart.

"The Heart"
Harvey Shapiro

I
Separate Blood

> Love comes from ferocious love
> or a ferocious lack of love, child.
>
> …To be home
> is to go somewhere, is velocity
>
> the same urgent comfort
> of your name.
>
> Brenda Shaughnessy

I CANNOT MAKE A TORCH OF GREEN BRANCHES

The living does not burn, even after
cold protests of smoke. Green branches
will not take a spark like the dead.

I cannot make a torch of skin and hair.
Not out of bones.
But burn an animal's fat, and a living blaze
will open the dark.

I divide a carcass for our meal
and blade the meat from tall
crevasses of sinew and fat that will melt
to unmake the lamb's body.

Would I know this texture if I quartered
my body, would I find I am run through
with what's ready to fire?

Or would I find the child in flesh and ropes,
in sieves and houses and blood?

Will I find her in this light by which
I read, by which I cook?
The lithe fire. The fire for hours.

A WOMB SOUND

Sometimes a sound, a womb sound.
Don't deny that the infant remembers:
the cut and tear that let in
the enormous light, the cut of cold

air to build her separate blood.
The infant from blanket of body
to a tub. A birth mother
from blanket of body to pitcher

poured out. And what dry,
dry mouths. What I have: the shape
of a milk vase, a wide-bottom curve
beneath parting lips, the shape

a hammer, the shape a leaf stem
just at release. On the bus,
a pregnant woman tells me her blood
volume has doubled, that now

she does nothing but sleep
and make protein. Did I take half
or give you twice more?
Before either could speak, we were

out of words. Do you go composing
a handful of sounds, a shout, a shout
swallowed? If you live by water
does it make all other rhythms

impossible? If silence can be measured
like length of rope, or hair, or neck,
what language would we find in the fold?
And then, what mouths?

A HOUSE OF PAPER AND GUT

You will be born in winter,
come steaming into the cold,
cold air, your little red
face more red against it.

I have neither honeycomb
nor nest. There is nothing of
my feathers in your bed.
I am not the burrowing animal

who claws a home, who chews
and tacks it together with her tongue.
I cannot bring from myself a house
of paper and gut.

You will come with much already
built, already to be torn down.
But we are not builders.
Look how we have made
you without any hands at all.

LOS ANGELES PASTORAL

> *I believed I could tame anything.*

In tall lot weeds, a still eye
swings from the cat's jaw,
eye still gazing, still hunted.
The cat smears my path
with blood and lust.
These weeds are full of beasts
and wild.

> *With nothing for instinct,*
> *I knew nothing of fear*

I chase away the soft
pressure of bees and moths
digging into every daisy's face,
every follicle stuck
deep with legs and hairs.
I cannot bear the hot
winging away of their powder.

> *or flight, or how the two*
> *sleep curled on the same*

All summer I fill a terrarium with spiders
but soon tire of catching their
meals. I release them
onto the road and watch their forelegs
scooping the white waves
of shimmering asphalt
as the terrible vibrations roll nearer.

> *side of the heart, one waking*
> *always the other.*

I collect no more after the frog

I cup from a pothole and raise
up to see how her marbled,
mottled skin perfectly mimics
the pattern of river stones.
She trembles under my breath,
and when her little running heart
catches itself,
she launches down onto a stone
on the flat of her back.

> *When I was afraid*

I see then the dozen tadpoles
navigating my foot's submerged
curves. And suddenly I know
all the ones pressed beneath me,
their tender weight,
my own tender branches
running with first sap.

> *I held still.*

THE SEA WALL

The wall breaks and enters
the sea, who swallows
the barrier fragment
and slips through the hole like an arm
through a dress sleeve, and smoothes
and smoothes the sleeve to
sand we stand on.
We die grain by grain.
How else to make salt
houses for all the creatures
who, as we cannot, go down and
down and open their eyes.

IN US THE UNUSED

The leopard can slay the furiously
angling gazelle, but not protect the kill.

So into the tree she drags herself
and the meat behind her. In her jaws

all strength converges to open the bag
of skin, the bags of blood,

then lash and gnaw the antler buds.
I eat watching the leopard feed,

knocking fork tines against my gums.

Her three cubs look exactly alike, exactly
like the mother as cub—their inheritance

whole. The leopard's blind infant
does not need to be told what it is.

In my mother, all the unused: the eye
color, the delicate chin no one will receive.

In her the coiling codes of instincts laid
dull, a stranger's yolk in the fretful

infant she accepts. What, if not blood,
if not body, does a daughter

receive to be called daughter? What if
I eat mother's language, mother's

melancholy, but never tasted milk?
Inside us, inheritance is a muscle

withered to water. And if one day I find
all muscle outmatched

by desire to bathe in oil and light,
desire to build a room around the dark?

Oh, but we have never stopped
eating in trees. What meat my jaws

ache after. What meat.

SUBJECT TO WIND

If let go, the kite becomes string and paper
litter. Tethered
—like the hawk, like the hound—

the kite remains
part of the arm, locked in the ball
rotation of the shoulder,

the finger
and the diamond on the same
strip of muscle.

The tethered thinks *escape*
while dragging its rope after
its neck,

and yet cannot see its body
is the rope.

What,
subject to the wind,
can think its own
release?

Where
can it head that the spinning
earth has not already been?

The kite is attached
to the father, a dragon
lolling over the cypresses.

The girl stands
below him so that he takes
up half the sky.

With each breath he
wolfs the air
and the string, the resistance,
the restraint.

INFERTILITY

There are many petals on the table.
A vase remains streaked with rot
from a dead ocean of stems that can
draw up no more. When I said *sunflowers*
thick and wide as something's wing,

she hoped they—those heavy heads
on failing necks—would be anything
else. My mother never liked flowers.
No fruit, she said, *ever comes*.

She liked less ones whose faces
turned to seed, these orphans cut from
their directive to fruit, spilling their
bloom onto the counter.

She clears more crumbled softness
each day, all the fallen reasons to bear
flowers at all, soon balding, sooner useless.

SPARROW

your wing-weight
is just enough
to mess your nest

I have brushed with
a human stain
the tight spotted

eggs you would
have fouled anyway
seeing now the crow

descend on your blue
brood and as they
fell you said

*before the stranger tries
to lie here I will unmake
this bed myself*

ON THE VINE

Strawberries emerge pale
before deepening in slow quadrants,
as if blood swells the heart. So fresh
in our basket, so open to sugar.

To plant again, we lay them loose
on a towel and sacrifice the fruit.
The directions are simple: leave the berries
to shrivel, then push the clots through a sieve.

The seeds catch. Rinse them free.
Pinch them into glycine bags so next year's ghosts
can grow under our gaze, so we don't miss the heart's
first throb, the first ripe rush and temptation.

OF WHAT NEXT

      You churn the earth and instructions
come. The seasons say.
Rain comes or delays.
      The sun is enough before it burns.

      You push and bend and cup.
You leave skin in the dirt.
      Late petals and leaves get eaten to webs.

      Something needs you, which is
the easy part. There is no question
of what next, of whether to grow.

      Respond to its need to be buried
and the garden stands up.

      You plant asclepias to call over
butterflies, and from everywhere they come.

You learn that something called
      will respond. Something urged turns
into something allowed.

      Look, out of this rocky sleeve of land
and a gauze of rain, out of your hands
      that separate thready stems, then bed

their eyelash roots—look how all
      you can do is put them deep and answer.

YOLK

When my mother asked
the fortuneteller to send
my grandfather's spirit home
to Hoi-Ping, the fortuneteller
asked for an egg.

My mother watched the old
man make the egg stand up.
His spirit in balance, she is told.
Protein and albumen equilibrium.

Fatherless and at peace, my mother
buries the egg in the yard.
The watery half-life inside
its cradle and coffin.

SWALLOWS IN HARBIN

No one knows what birds can remember.
And yet, to every house
two always return, mouths full of nesting
glue from blue island wintering.

Villagers clear windows and rafters
for another year's pair. And if
the swallows are late, so is the planting,
so the entire season.

A year's length is measured in scythes
of returning wings.
A year stretches or recoils
awaiting a flock's trumpeting approach.

Each day the heart slows and releases
its time. Each sunrise takes its minutes.
And if a body gives in to delay, the late
sewn rice still uncoils its reed, the grain

still starches the belly, and still a body
can lie down in provincial dusk,
a few minutes gathered
or scattered into the rows it digs.

WHY WE ARE THIS WAY

Because my mother cannot remember
the churn of revolution around her,
because she could never, even after six

trips to China, find her father's ghost,
she brought me there to help her look.

Because she could not bring a child
from herself, she brought one across the ocean
and we are both immigrants now.

Because she needed a child without memory
of blood or hunger, she bought too much milk

only to realize a baby needs formula,
only to try to save the milk by freezing it,

only to have it thaw and separate like overcooked
meat from its bone.

Because I never felt the sea beneath me,
because I was not carried across its back but
hurled in jet stream, because I was not running

I was arriving, she didn't know what to say
when we first met.

Because in every dream she is a forest of doors
batting against a forest of hinges, and in every dream

I am every wave shouting endlessly that I, too,
have an old taste of salt,
my eyes ablaze and my tongue rotten with it.

Because she came by boat with her own mother,
now immigration is the only thing she knows
of mothers and daughters.

Because, in China again this summer, she takes
the flashy bus tours and stays in the most

Western hotels, because in a name tag and hat
she can return and return and never return
to where she was born, where she should not have

to quarry the ruins of her mother tongue
just to speak to strangers.

Because now my hips are crooked, my belly
soft and rippled from the girl
I carried, I have done yet another thing she could never.

Because I speak and she speaks and neither can listen
in the other language or silence our own because,

without words, what would we then have to know?

A PHRASE BY ROTE

You take your eyes off
the water, off whether

I go or am taken,
whether I swim along

or away from shore.
When my feet no longer
stand me

on the slick grave of shells,
my body, to the neck,
is the water.

The lie is that we
are lighter than water,

that we would not sink
even if left to.

When all we do is churn
to keep the air in, surging
to stay upward

long after having forgotten
how to crawl.

My toe opens
against some shard
or shell, and salt

rushes the wound as blood
rushes out.

The two forces of liquid don't
cancel each other.

I am a little
phrase of music, the chorus
and verse of a hand's

muscle memory
learning the pull

of land against ocean's
tongue. I ask return
as coin or drift

of softened glass.
None of this you
see, there on a blanket

on a chair, refusing
the sun's bath in your

long sleeves,
in your story's sealess world.
A collection of vessels

wrecks in my throat.
My blood stain reveals

all the bleached
towel's independent
threads, tamed and crossed—

reveal how, out of raw
fiber, fabric is made

from two directions.
The way waves upend
direction and throw

water down my lungs
so I can't say the sky

is not blasting me
the same as sea:

this way I will
remember a phrase
by rote:

All things
disaster
sooner or later.

AN EYE TO SEE

How the horse ripples his back to scatter
flies that zero back unafraid. The brave
drink his eyes and sauna under his nostril.

The horse could stand all day shivering all
over, but better to let them have him
than seize for half a moment's relief.

Before begging off a great humid lung
or kneeling by this blinking lake to tongue
its oily tears, the fly once pumped the world

through his body. Which knows enough to pay
the other any attention, which knows
enough to ignore? Even ignoring

imagines eyes turned *somewhere*. Neither does
the dream ever change: see me through
and through, every scrap and repair, every

frayed stitch of a heartbeat. Indifferent
muscles under bristling hairs, unworried
kaleidoscope eyes over wings: how would

either say to the other, *there you are.*
Long before eyes, chambers grow to house them.
This fallow field never not an empty
socket waiting to see us for itself.

GRAVID

You swim in me to feed and breathe.
The gulps of fluid in your lungs are

your lungs. Into them: what has
already traveled me. If I breathe

a stamen, you are stamen.
If I taste bitter salt, you are char

and ash. What do you take
when I take in another's body,

when I soak my neck in oil that sings
gardenia but is not flower?

The journey inside me has
something to do with blood,

carrying on it like barges the wide outside
you already taste, and all you will soon see.

I suck this sodden spring air down to you
and everything is dying.

Everything is beginning to loosen, drop
its seeds and say *what's needed is done.*

They come up from the ground, these shoots.
They come out of the trees, these flowers to fruit,

and the air parts for them, the fired dirt
swaddles the ready germ.

There is so much ahead now, there is only
time to unravel, to say *what next*.

Your cells are dividing to build you, and yet, like
the rest of us, you begin dying too.

We take our time, and while we gorge on,
what we have eaten is eaten forever.

II
Bone

> Who can tell what metals the gods use in forging the subtle bond which we call sympathy, which we might as well call love.
>
> Kate Chopin

GO BACK, MAKE READY

1.
My girl is born and then I follow
outside myself. A latch slides
and clicks into place
in the gray squall and spray.

When I was born, I emptied a mother out
and went to live in my body.

She shuffled her vacant room
back down to size.

2.
The mother who received me
long called herself empty.
She filled me up with soup and meat,
filled herself with who I was
supposed to be.

3.
Another girl and we are four.
She, too, cut from the opening sharp
but not straight,
the same one closed two years before.

We know only two things:
damage and repair.

4.
In this birthlight, all I can remember is
I was born and now I am open.

I am the sum of some breaths.

5.
The doctor pinches my skin in place,
traces the tight tissue crater
above reattached passages. Feeling may
never return, never certain
about sliced nerves.

My dark ravine remembers the stitches
beneath, on each organ and sac
cut to make her a corridor.

6.
Repair is made from *go back*
and *make ready*. Go back to her
fluid room.
Go back to a wedding
day, to the sign that no
one will make a home inside her.
Go back to the fall of a whole
life out with its own cord and cry.

Go back to first
desires and make ready.

7.
Her little gleaming body has never
harmed anything, yet I am
a throbbing tear, a swollen scar,
an evacuated ballroom.
She has not done this to me.

And yet what did.

8.
How dry the skin over hot
milk, how small
the layer between liquid and air.

The nursling grows
tender on her bones.

9.
My mother has never had a surgery
or sonogram.
My mother's body is soft with
more corners than walls.
She fixes clothes for size and signs
of wear.

The garment dragging behind me
betrays a fray in every seam.

10.
The mittens muffle her
sharp newborn reflexes. Diaphragm
spasms her sleep with laughter,
a current spikes her
arms to surrender. Her tongue
lashes the air but no tears fall,

just an alarm, then mewling gulps
that say repair has begun.

THE DEAD IN DAYLIGHT

Dreams and the dead are for daylight.
If in the dark a dream tries to walk

through my mouth, I bite it back.
If the dream escapes, it will grow

legs and strangle me.
If the dead open my eyes,

I lead them by the hand outside,
where my mother exiles snakes

of incense ash, rotted ancestor
fruit, and clipped hair.

In mourning, before a funeral,
do not walk through anyone's door.
Do not curse a good home with your
white arm band.

We build no houses for the dead
so they come lie with me, staining

me with inky breath. When my mother asks
why I am crying, I tell her a bad dream.

The moon brightens her dread.

In the darkness, I speak dark things.
So she hurries from my room.

On a holiday, do not sweep. Do not bathe.
Do not extinguish your porch light.
Let the fortune see you and cling to your oily head.

We bow and cajole. We keep arms
length and spirits sedated.

In the morning, palm shadows still look
like a wide wind chime of blades.

My mother sees night clinging to me.
Mho gong. Do not talk. We eat instead.

A bowl of rice noodles and scrap meat
she chews and chews.

Do not buy a house at the mouth of a street.
The mouth will open and swallow all your
neighbors' misfortune.

Her fear commands, be invisible
to disaster. I hide well from the dead

and the living, who are everywhere too.
I skip my baths and the layers rise,

grease and sweat mudded with every
speck of luck my stink lures.

Before leaving home, I show
the dead my dream of stones

abrading the grime of fortune's bait
to exhume a visible shine.

TRAILS

In famine, roads evaporate
        with no one to trample them
                to road anymore.
Thirst disappears a country.

Hauling rags to town, my grandmother
        cannot distinguish her path
                from the dismantled land.

She gnaws a bundle of sugarcane
        scraps, but only
                one end of every fibrous cigar.

Each day, she walks to where people
        gather to make fires,
                and offers to mend. Even in
blight, people must dress.

My grandmother sucks what
        she can, then fans each wet,
                unraveled cane end to a flare,

a brush head. She points
        the burst ends toward home
                and drops one every twenty steps.

She will never read of birds
        who steal breadcrumbs and leave
children stranded in woods to resist
                soft ginger walls.

        Would that there were any woods
My grandmother will know nothing of quiet
      words on pages. All her stories

brimming on her body.
        She will leave trails of jewelry bribes
for the boatmen, trails of churning

      currents under frail sea legs,
trails of her own tongue
      crumbled to birds.

What course can be laid without scraps,
      without an ushering hand and
a secret map for hunger?

OVERWINTERING

What strand of mandevilla does not reach
blue flower, we cut.
And we cut the ones full or nearing bloom.

To overwinter, we hang the shrubs bald
and upside down in the dark.

Some life remains to drink
a gallon every two weeks. By March,
they will take soil again.

Perhaps neither they nor we should grow
where we cannot shorten our own roots.

Perhaps there are mouths of land we cannot
have if we cannot scale back our branches
or seal our own cracks.

Already we know we cannot slow
our pulse to wait out hunger.
Our young cry in all seasons.

Neither can the mandevilla stop
sending flowers to bud, even into

the iced air, even for fear
that every petal will release and make
no mark where it lands.

RHYTHMS

The house hums its works.
Its pumps and jolts for light
and heat. My body rhythms
itself to the machines
and his breaths as I
search for sleep, until a cry
churns me up to close
her to my chest, to pat
a rhythm of shush on her back,
as she learns to warm
and calm herself.
In the house there is never
not a noise. Never not
a vessel filling to empty,
a current not cooling, a moss
not creeping its glacial creep while
we cling to our bones,
always inside everyone's
shaky song, every unrowed stroke
of our basic heartbeat.

A SEA BENEATH SKIMMING BIRDS

The father does not remove bones
from his own bowl of fish.

The father, not immigrant, has a straight
tongue always in the right place.

The father speaks the daughter's language,
two broken wings on the same bird.

The father unafraid looks like he lacks
sense, but what he lacks is grief.

The father was not fathered and so clings to
charming colorful harmless boyhood things.

When the father surveys a day, or table, or lifetime,
he asks nothing more than exactly what is there.

The father's roads are ground to pearl, and he
is often silent when he thinks he is speaking.

The father was a listening child, listening to
women cleaver, soak, and season history.

The father puts his wants in others' mouths, says
you like this instead of *please*.

The father likes his eggs wet and runny, but no one
cooks them this way so he never eats them this way.

The father, a sea beneath skimming birds with
wings enough to stray one day's hunger from land.

ALL THE LETTERS

In my dream, our girl gets lost and becomes
someone else's.
In the dream, no one understands her little
babbles or pointing cries
so she learns new ones.
She is my grandfather sent from China at
twelve, who lost
all the years in Cantonese.
My dream ends when our girl comes
back and I cannot understand
anything she says.
I hoard memories neither girl nor grandfather
has any use for,
all while my lips tremble with lack
and all the letters
each must still learn.

OPEN FIELD AND MIRROR

My mother says *I love you*
to my daughter
when my daughter
will not play with her.
I love you across the room
to a toddler on froggy knees.
My daughter does not need
my mother to love her,
does not take care to avoid
sharpness against my mother's
curve of glass, even if just to hear
the clear, high note.
My mother says *I love you*
as a plea, *I love you* as a sigh.
As *oh, well*.
After a while, my daughter
beams her face toward me.
It opens to let
light onto my craggy cliff.
It will see to return
me to myself.
Each day, I beckon and beg
her warm glow, her wide
open field and mirror.
I love you as promise,
I love you as medicine,
I love you as bailer for the slow
steady leak.

THE CHAIN FOLLOWS THE LIGHT

The cormorant
dives and throats a pike that cannot slip past
the red twine knot
blocking the path down to its ready, roiling belly.

The cormorant with tucked blue metal wings
lets the fisherman massage the fish
out of its gullet.

An engine of instincts
plunges the cormorant after its darting targets.
A hand-raised life
nurtures duty to another's need, trains delivery of each
gasping catch onto the boat floor.

The hunter who cannot sate himself
waits for permission.
Basket filled, the fisherman cuts
the red collar
and rewards the bird with a muddy bottom-dweller.

Their dance carries into dark. The bird receives some
music, the river skimmed
with feet and oars, the river rattled with bounty songs.

To fish after dusk, oil lanterns lure a swirl of easy targets.
What do fish know of fire
to be hypnotized out of the muck?

But lights only draw the food, the little plankton
thinking they see
sun and charging their hunger upward.
And then the whole food chain follows in a dead
of night hunt,

first little slips of fish raking up the microscopic zoo,
then hunters, and their hunters
and their guardians. The river teeming petition,
offering and claim.

AS IF
        after The Book of Odes, #55

as if uncut, as if raw
as if guest flesh could be claimed by host
how rendered, how remaindered

as if worms burrowing, as if at the center
they knew such a center

as if wood or womb, as if in birth
there is no grief
how either, how nothing

and then a boat, as if a boat
could carry without resistance

as if the world had edge,
as if new life were not also a grief

as if unchiseled, as if unpolished
as if love could be error

as if beckoned, as if followed
as if the erasure were a road

as if running, as if always toward

OR AM I

A curtain of starlings rises from wheat.
They spread to a sheet, then close as if
a single fist, a patternless organ

pumping toward the road.
At the corner of my headlights,
a storm of black and green flashing

eyes upon feathers. How close the glass
and metal hum between us.
How close I come to covering my eyes.

You and I are nothing like starlings,
neither apace in blood rhythm
nor breath. My body makes a room for you,

a brush stroke, a blue light.
In the end, a combine will churn
you up from my field.

I dream a crush of starlings between my legs.
Are you the shifting mass, or am I?
Are you the murmur of dusk, or am I?

Are you the one bird in the body who sees
the light nearing and makes the first turn?
Are you the spilling sidewing beast

swallowing the falcon, or am I?

THE FATHER COLLAPSES

During the dishes, his eyes close.
His body lightens and loosens
its control of fluids.
Nothing wrong, they say.
The spot beneath the sink
has dried. The towels
are arranged again.
My mother does not tell him
how long he took to wake.
He does not know where his favorite
jeans have gone. I feel
the same, he insists, but he is
chastened, his arrogance dimmed.
A little slip away, a sudsy dream
of what remains, leaves him
a little less. I slap his hand away from
heavy bags, the door,
the steering wheel.
My daughters are stretching
out, out, away, some days
punching their way free.
My father is unlocking
his limbs for me to fold under
the swaddle, is waiting to be
lifted and brought near.

BAT EXCLUSION

All August, our house drips
with bats' oily bodies
slung everywhere like leather fruit.
Our house a sudden orchard.

We learn there are young tucked above
the porch's bead board.
That where they are born

will echo all their lives.
No matter the shelter of southern caves
full of water-grazing insects,

our dim, exposed porch is forever
where these missiles home in.

I read that they can hang from
a scratch in a light bulb.
They can alight thin as a line.

Three men seal every crack around
escape tubes that prevent reentry.
The grease records silent exile.

The men say, expect the babies
to return for five seasons.

Shedding their winter caves
they will make a miniature
migration to city parks and rafters.

They will always find their first place,
but will move on when locked out.
Experience will finally tell them

abandon the empty echo, every call
returns the same knowledge;
you could wait for it, but don't.

HEAR HER SAY EVERYTHING

      Begin with the mother,
the second mother.
Both she and the first
      asked for another life.

Begin your new home
against memory. You're home as
long as you carry nothing.
                     Except

you look exactly like her.
Begin to understand what
mother means.

      Begin feeding the new
mother as soon as you meet.

A daughter is sustenance
but not food.
      She is ration.

      Hungrier than anyone
is the mother full of alarm,

the mother braced for loss.
And the other unbracing.

      Begin your first feeding.
Begin to fill your always
asking bird mouth.

      What is it
you want with so much?

Begin to feed your own girls when
they say hungry, even

when you know they mean
some other kind.

       Begin the question
unanswered because never asked.

Begin the ocean string and beat.
Begin the throat shiver of music.

Begin as if words say.

       Begin to know that she is
afraid of you.
       Her powerlessness empties

her eyes as fast as your careless
temptations of bad luck,

faster than your fast English talk
you know she cannot catch.
                       You,

the abandoned, shadow
her with abandonment.

          Begin again
the dream of stitching
the cord back. Begin as if you could
name all she had missed.

Begin the longest night
with the question,
what do you want from me?
              Begin to hear her answer.

Begin to hear her say everything,
that she wants everything.

She stands on shore, looking
at your foreign land.
        Begin to repair a lighthouse

for her, to signal in
        pulses, in darkness.

A STORY OF BONE

When an animal dies at sea, the body
usually sinks to rot and feed.

But if enough sediment falls on its bones
before they splinter to silt, if enough

pressure and heat close in and begin
forming a flesh of rock around them,

then the captured bones, pressed
like a prize in the layers, will leave

their shape inside the ocean floor long
after the living material dissolves.

My mother made it across the ocean.
She sank into the California loam,

her knees and teeth rubbled.
A fossil forms when minerals clot

in trapped bone or hollow mold
to forge an impossibly new

and ancient cast copy, a precise living
shadow. My mother touched like

onyx, like opal, like ivory. She braced herself
long against sea bloat and toss, perhaps

never to unclench. Or perhaps she let
what she must encase her living

form and replace it with some
other deposit after she washed away.

Shifting plates plunge beneath each
other, or part, or grind their edges

for eons. Then a fault invites seeping
light, which only such breaks allow.

Melody S. Gee was born in Taiwan and raised in Cerritos, California. Her first poetry collection, *Each Crumbling House*, won the 2010 Perugia Press Book Prize. Recent poems and essays appear in *Copper Nickel, The Book of Scented Things Anthology, Spillway,* and *Boxcar Poetry Review*. She holds degrees in English from the University of California Berkeley and the University of New Mexico, and has been awarded a Robert Watson Literary Prize and a Kundiman Poetry Retreat Fellowship. Currently, she teaches developmental writing at St. Louis Community College, and lives with her husband and two daughters in Missouri. Find her online at www.melodygee.com

www.ingramcontent.com/pod-product-compliance
Lightning Source LLC
Chambersburg PA
CBHW020035120526
44588CB00031B/806